QUIET MOMENTS
With Benedict Groeschel

QUIET MOMENTS
With Benedict Groeschel

120 DAILY READINGS

Compiled by the
Editors of Servant Publications

CHARIS

SERVANT PUBLICATIONS
ANN ARBOR, MICHIGAN

© 2000 by Servant Publications

Charis Books is an imprint of Servant Publications especially designed to serve
Roman Catholics.

Published by Servant Publications
P.O. Box 8617
Ann Arbor, Michigan 48107

Cover design: DesignTeam, Grand Rapids, Michigan

00 01 02 03   10 9 8 7 6 5 4 3

Printed in the United States of America
ISBN 0-56955-209-6

LIBRARY OF CONGRESS CATALOGING-IN-PUBLICATION DATA

Groeschel, Benedict J.
   Quiet moments with Benedict Groeschel : 120 daily readings / compiled
by the editors of Servant Publications.
     p.   cm.
Includes bibliographical references.
ISBN 1-56955-209-6 (alk. paper)
1. Meditations.   2. Catholic Church—Prayer-books and devotions—
English.   3. Devotional calendars.   I. Servant Books (Firm)   II. Title.

BX2182.2.G76   2000
242'.2—dc21   00-031569

Introduction

Priest. Psychology professor. Popular speaker and writer. Pastor of the poor. Protector of the young. They're all in one intriguing package named Benedict Groeschel—affectionately called Father Benedict.

Father Benedict draws his readers to a mature faith and holy living—always in a compassionate voice mellowed by years of ministry with troubled youth and needy families in the South Bronx, near the Capuchin-style community he helped to found, the Franciscan Friars of the Renewal.

He's a clear teacher, an animated storyteller, and a keen spiritual guide who laces his writing with subtle humor, as in the selection titled "The Geographic Cure": "Have you ever tried the 'geographic cure' for some chronic problem like alcoholism or depression—that is, changing jobs or moving to another city? The problem is, you have to take yourself along with you." He calls his readers to personal reform—never in and by their own power but always with and by the empowering Spirit of God.

Whether you are familiar with his work or just browsing for a stimulating spiritual read, we invite you to delight in this collection, each selection chosen for its provocative spiritual and psychological insight.

1. Give Me Your Gifts

Give me your gifts and lift me up, O Holy Spirit, my Advocate promised to me by Christ himself. I am often cast down, defeated, and broken; often blind and insensitive even to those I love; often caught up foolishly in that which is passing away before my eyes. Spirit of truth, when this road is long and weary and I am fearful and tired, lift me up on your eagle wings so that I may not fail utterly those whom you have given me in this life to influence, to help and to support. Give me your wisdom at every stage of my journey that I may know that you alone make all things new and good and beautiful. Then I shall be a blessing to others and cease to be an obstacle to them and a burden to myself.

2. Even the Dimmest Candle

Light is an especially potent symbol. How utterly dark this world would be without the illumination that God provides. Imagine descending into the deepest coal mine, surrounded by pitch black. The only way your eyes could penetrate the darkness closing in upon you would be by means of the small lamp attached to your miner's hat....

I think divine illumination operates in our spiritual lives in somewhat the same way as a single candle. God promises to shine his light on our pathway, but usually only a few steps ahead at a time. Although on rare occasions a floodlight may break through our fleshly fog, we tend to complain that we've been given only flashlights—with batteries that seem to go dead right at crucial moments! But we don't necessarily need searchlights or laser beams to make progress on our spiritual journey. God is able to use even the dimmest candlelight to illuminate the path ahead.

3. Let Me Welcome You

O Lord Jesus Christ, give me the grace to become your true disciple. Let me see ever more clearly that faith in you is not simply a conviction of my mind—but a call to live my life for you and with you.

Your presence as Son of God is all around me ... in the sacraments, in the Scripture, in the poor and suffering, in the lowly and the dying, even among your enemies where you are betrayed and crucified anew. Send your Holy Spirit to tear aside the veil of material appearances so that I may grow ever more aware of your presence all around me.

Let me welcome you into the center of my poor being just as you came to the house of the publican. Let me seek and find you, recognize and serve you in all who suffer. Give me the grace, O Savior of the world, to bring your presence even to your enemies and to persist faithfully in witnessing to them even when I find it painful to do so. Let me be inspired by your martyrs who constantly call us back to you, our only hope and salvation.

4. Lifted on the Wings of Grace

We may say that the river of life's events provides a most powerful impetus for prayer. In the din of life he speaks to us, calls to us and providentially provides the materials of our salvation. We cannot tap this great stream in which grace unfolds unless we receive God's help.... It is a valuable tool in the life of the spirit to pause and ask for the grace of prayer.

Human beings in all their religions have paused to pray in the morning and evening, to begin and end the day of conscious awareness with a prayer. The person interested in a life of prayer should take advantage of these two natural periods of rest to ask the help of the Lord to sanctify the day by listening to his voice.

We need help to surrender our preconceived notions and fantasies, to go beyond our defenses and shallow expectations, to be lifted on the eagle wings of grace. To the one who seeks, it will be given; to the one who knocks, it shall be opened; to the one who listens, it shall be revealed.

5. Let Me Be Willing

O Holy Spirit, when I met those who were truly blessed, the pure of heart and humble of mind, the real peacemakers who loved in the face of hate, have I recognized and acknowledged in them the greatest of all your works? Have I listened attentively as the unseen and unknown martyrs and confessors praise you even in this world? Have I joined them, however weakly, in their chorus of praise ... or have I listened more clearly to sounding brass and clanging cymbals?

When, O Lord, when shall I love you and all others in you? When shall I desire you as the deer pants for running streams? When shall I let my soul be raised on eagle's wings? No, O Lord, this is not the real question; this is not the best prayer. Teach me that wherever I am, I shall take the next good step on the journey to you. Let me be willing to do what is most real: to hear you as you stand and knock in the reality of NOW, and of HERE, where I stand ready to take the next good step toward you; and with your continued help, to take the next, and the next.

6. Open to the Mystery

B.F. Skinner shortly before his death wrote ... that for years he had pretended to be an atheist because he did not know what to do with God. Finally, as the end of his life approached, he expressed his conviction that God exists, and even returned to the radical Protestantism of his youth. All those years this very bright man had been doing what so many others do—he was running away from mystery by pretending it did not exist.

Unlike Skinner and many others, some of us could not run away from these mysteries.... At a very distinct moment in the second grade, in the parish church of Our Lady of Victory in Jersey City, I knew that I was supposed to be a priest. A vocation, a mysterious call, was there from that moment. I did not become a priest because of an intuition of mystery but because of a grace or gift from God. It was there. Bang! But this vocation—or conviction (it is clearer and more permanent than any other conviction I have ever had)—opened my mind to mystery and to the need to explore mysteries of faith.

7. Christian Conversion

"The time is fulfilled, and the kingdom of God is at hand; repent, and believe in the gospel" (Mk 1:15, RSV). Conversion, or *metanoia,* as the Greek New Testament refers to it, is the first real experience of the Christian spiritual life. For some who have grown up in a devout home and have never deviated much from Christ's teaching, conversion takes on more the aspect of an awakening, like the call of Nathanael, who was asleep under a tree and whom our Lord called a man without guile. Others, who have never really been active disciples even though they were baptized, or who have simply had no relation to the Gospel at all and are unbaptized, may experience a conversion that affects every level of their lives. If their conversion is authentically spiritual, it will be experiential (affecting how they perceive things), theological (affecting what they believe), moral (affecting what they do), and even emotional (affecting what they feel). In the beginning of a conversion, the emotional and spiritual are so close to each other that they are experienced as the same thing. In time a wise person will come to see that they are not identical at all.

8. How Patient? How Merciful?

A few of us, at certain grace-filled moments, may imagine that we possess infinite patience. This is an illusion. And if you know some patient, loving Christian soul, you might want to try the "pass the butter test" to see how infinite that patience really is.

Here's how the "butter test" works. Serve a fluffy baked potato or fresh corn on the cob or homemade rolls for dinner. Instruct everyone at the table (except the one who is to be your test subject) to respond appropriately to all requests from that test subject, except when he or she asks for the butter. Tell them to ignore that particular request, as if they hadn't heard a thing.

Test subjects basking in the advanced stages of the illuminative way usually make it to about the fifth query before they turn the whole table upside down or lunge for the butter in a "boarding house reach"....

Mercy characterizes our lives in much the same way as patience: more the exception than the norm. Does God expect *us* to be everlasting in mercy? I suspect not. "Blessed are the merciful" simply calls us to do a better job of practicing mercy.

9. Listening to Life

The following event provided me with a moving example of a person who had almost no intellectual understanding of prayer, but who listened and then prayed. I once visited a man in a leper colony.... When we came to the man's tiny cottage, I discovered that leprosy had destroyed not only his hands but also his eyes and most of his face. Yet he was a happy, peaceful man. He told us he was grateful to have contracted the disease because when he was well he had led a wild, dissipated life; now he was seeking God and was filled with peace. No one looking on this frightful illness and hearing the tone of his simple statement could doubt that the man's words reflected his true state of mind. I was deeply moved as he touched his little statue of the Madonna and Child with the stump of his arm and told us of his devotion to the Mother of Christ. He was indeed a happy man. He had been able to pray with life because he had listened to it first.

10. Do We Care?

With the little bit of creation that God has given you, how do you protect it, care for it, cherish it, love it? Do you see God in creation; do you pause to see him in the glory of the sky, the magnificence of nature? Do you see the tragedy of evil in children led into delinquency and sin? Are you concerned about people who starve?... In a word, do you care? Do I care? To come to any realization of a Creator is to bring into our own heart the idea that ... after we look at the entire world, we must see it is guided by a knowing mind. If you do this you are then approaching belief. It goes beyond demonstration. There is no other answer, but this answer must be accepted by belief. Belief is a gift which the Creator gives to the creature so that he can be known.... One does not come to believe by simply willing to believe.... Faith is when God reaches out to you and to me and we reach back.

II. Discipleship and Community

To be disciples of Christ, we must be part of a praying community. The distinguished Anglican, Evelyn Underhill, writes that the founders of the world religions either started a prayer community or already belonged to one. Our Lord belonged to one such praying community, that of the Jews. We sometimes forget that Jesus was a Jew to the core. A community, Underhill suggests, keeps disciples on a realistic spiritual road. Our Lord did not need a community, but he realized that his followers did.

Thus our Lord started a new praying community which came to be known as Christianity. Jesus was not a lone ranger. He gathered around himself a small band of twelve apostles, as well as a larger community of disciples. His followers strengthened him in his own daily struggle of obedience to the Father, while at the same time they received from him the spiritual formation to carry on after his crucifixion.

12. Beyond Reform?

It should come as no surprise that constant repentance, the regretful acknowledgment of sin, is one of two essential components of the Christian life. It also is clear that reform, the positive effort to change and overcome our tendency toward evil, is the cutting edge of an integrated Christian life. Those who pretend that the community of followers of Christ is perfect have neglected to take into account this important fact of life. Christ never claimed that his followers would be perfect, that is, beyond repentance and reform. The vacillating fisherman whom Christ chose to be the leader of his community is a compelling example of this. The Gospels recount Peter's constant falls and temptations, and Tradition suggests that his wavering continued to the end of his life. Awareness of the need for reform is simply the reflection of the conflict between time and eternity, between the self-seeking and self-transcendental.

13. We Need the Gift of Courage

We all need the gift of courage in our quest for righteousness. Courage comes in big bites and little bites, whatever we need to overcome our own personal obstacles. But first we have to be hungry enough to ask for it.

In English, the word "courage" usually connotes the ability to stand up in the midst of a particular danger. But in the Romance languages, it suggests a whole attitude toward life—a certain enthusiastic or at least persistent determination in the face of all obstacles. The latter definition is closer to the meaning of this marvelous gift of the Holy Spirit which gives us the strength to face even the most difficult challenges of life.

Courage is a natural human quality, which by grace can be raised to a Christian virtue. It is also a gift of the Holy Spirit which enables us to endure much for the kingdom of God—even if we aren't exactly courageous people. The virtue of courage can make a brave person good (and not all of them are), but the gift of the Holy Spirit, the gift of courage, can even make a cowardly person brave.

14. Prayer for Courage

Spirit of fire and truth, Holy Spirit of courage and fortitude, if I am honest with myself I do not really want too much of your gifts. I would like enough courage to make others admire me but I shrink from any courage that would make them disagree with me or despise me. Overcome my weakness and cowardice and feed my soul with your rich and insatiable hunger for righteousness. Satisfy my needs in this earthly life not with fulfillment but with an ever increasing desire to seek your justice and righteousness in the everyday world around me.

If I cannot find you among the real needs of real people, then I cannot find you at all and I shall remain forever unsatisfied. Give to your people your gift of courage, that we may hunger and thirst insatiably in this world. Then we may surely drink from your everlasting springs in the next.

15. Mary's Consent

Salvation would be God's gift, but it had to be accepted. It had been lost by the first parents of the human race, mysteriously described in the events of the Book of Genesis, and it would be recovered by the free consent of the human being who would accept the absolute salvation of God.

It is fruitful to meditate on the fact that this event took place in the most silent of ways. Just as no one had ever heard the explosion that was the "big bang," just as no one hears the cosmic events in the sky because they go on in a world where there are no ears to hear them, so also the event that would be the re-creation of the world took place in the absolute silence of the inner being of a single human.

The Gospel of St. Luke describes this event which is the second creation of the world. It is as mysterious and spellbinding, as utterly overpowering to the human intellect as the great explosion at the beginning of creation. But this time it includes the freedom of the human will. The human will had once chosen evil, now it would choose good.

16. Mary in Bethlehem

Nature calls all decent human beings to go beyond the narrow limits of self-preoccupation. Especially in parenting, nature calls for a suspension of the impulse to put oneself first that is so much a part of our way of thinking. The mother of the King of Kings, the King who Isaiah said would rule the nations, could have expected better treatment, a more dignified and comfortable birthplace than a manger for animals. But this mother is filled with joyful self-giving. She rejoices in her little mysterious son.

The strange and mysterious circumstances of his birth (to many they would have seemed degrading) remind Mary of something else as she rejoices and proclaims the goodness of the Lord: The Messiah is not only the King of Kings of the psalms but he is also the Suffering Servant of Isaiah. As will happen in all the profound mysteries of her life, Mary forgets herself in Bethlehem.

Do we forget ourselves as we experience grace amid the mysterious events of life? Some of these events can be confusing and some very painful.

17. We Are Not Poor

St. John of the Cross teaches that the sun, the moon, the stars, the earth, the sea, time, eternity, and the Mother of God all belong to us. We can't be poor. We can't be completely unfortunate. We have the angels and the saints for friends. Who owns the earth? Our heavenly Father. We are not poor. Worldly, unbelieving, grasping, manipulative people—they are the poor ones. They've invested their lives in junk. Invest your life in eternity if you are a believer. Note that those who are wealthy and are real believers act the same way as the other believers do. They are generous with what they have. They keep before their eyes very clearly that they will take with them only what they have given away.

18. Our Creator Is Our Redeemer

My Redeemer—your Redeemer—has the right to be called that because he suffered with us as well as for us. God could have saved us in some simpler, less terrible way than subjecting himself to the worst that human beings could do, but he wanted us to know how much he loved us when we are in pain and suffering. Salvation surely did not need to come through the murder of the Messiah. But that's how it came, so we could know, in all sufferings and sorrows of life, that our Creator was also our Redeemer, that he would bring joy out of sorrow, hope out of despair, love out of hate, life out of death, eternity out of time. This is our hope. It alone makes sense.

19. Christ, You Alone Know

O Lord Jesus Christ, you alone know the holiness of God and the weakness of humanity. You alone have dwelt in the heavens and on the earth. Though without sin, you have borne our infirmities and tasted the bitter effects of our evil deeds. You call us to be holy so that we may pass on to that holy life which is without any change or sorrow, to that place of endless day where there is no mourning or crying anymore. You have gone before us and sent the Advocate to stand beside us in our trials.

O Divine Master, call us ever more powerfully to follow you on the way of holiness. Call us to sanctification by your life and death, by your Word and sacraments. Save those who are dear to us. Save those who have strayed away. Call to those who are perishing because you have died for us all. And make us by your grace witnesses to your salvation and holiness in this world in which we struggle on, guided by the light shining from your cross.

20. The Last Words of St. Francis

I once sat in a totally unpredictable place talking to a person who has accomplished completely unexpected things for the kingdom of God. Mother Angelica, a cloistered Poor Clare, has developed a satellite television network, EWTN, adjacent to her convent in Birmingham, Alabama. With no regular source of income she provides religious television every day to millions of homes. Mother Angelica frightened me out of my wits by confiding, "Often, in the gray light of dawn, a chill comes over me. I ask what more I could have done if I had really trusted God." At first I thought that this was a touching humility, but as I thought about it I realized that she was right. We can always do more if we try to push back the limitations set by our own fears and shame.

Clare of Assisi no doubt heard from the friars the account of the last words of St. Francis, "Let us begin now, because so far we have done nothing." She did begin again. So can I. So can you.

21. Measure Meekness

I would encourage you to nurture the two obvious aspects of meekness—humbly accepting God's will and practicing moderation in your own needs and demands. Ask yourself these questions as a way to measure meekness in your own life:

1. Are you willing to accept where God has placed you, to be at peace with it, and to do the best you can wherever you are?

2. Are you a person of moderation, one who doesn't do anything to such an excess that you unduly become a cause of discomfort for others?

3. Are you willing in imitation of Christ to surrender even moderation in favor of self-denial when you face the demands of justice or of Christian charity?

As you make these two qualities your aim—especially the acceptance of God's will—you will find yourself advancing in the spiritual life. You will experience a deepening inner composure that helps you to pray and to do the will of God. And you will gradually experience more of God's light illuminating the pathway of your own spiritual journey.

22. The Witness of Generosity

The obvious way out of materialism is generosity—starting with almsgiving to the poor and going on to many other acts of kindness. The Gospels, the Epistles, and the lives of the saints from the earliest times until now offer a continuous call to generous giving. Many [priests] object that they have been taken advantage of by panhandlers at the door. This kind of incident represents only a small part of a Christian's obligation to be generous. In almost every parish, and certainly in every diocese, there are poor but gifted youngsters who need a better education than they are getting. There are needy elderly people who are on fixed incomes and families devastated by illness and death. There are immigrants and refugees who need the first boost up the ladder. Some will be grateful, and some will not. It makes no difference to the person seeking to grow in a spirit of repentance. How powerful a witness is a generous priest or minister! The most important thing for a generous clergyman to have is the willingness to open his eyes to see the needs of others in front of him.

23. Don't Be Quick to Judge

Often, persecution stems from basic prejudice—making a prejudgment or judging without the facts. We rush to judgment because of a person's name or nationality or color or religion, without pausing to check out reality or take a close look at the truth....

One person says, "I get sick when I hear about people who like to have Mass in Latin now and then." Others complain, "I hate hearing guitars in church. It's all New Age music." Prejudgment! We all have a right to enjoy whatever we happen to appreciate, as long as it's not sinful. But all sorts of people make up their minds beforehand about what's going to be good for *us*. Or we make up our minds for *them*....

But I have had prejudiced thoughts too. In England I saw a teenage youth with green hair. I became very annoyed. But how would I know why he chose to dye his hair green? Perhaps he was an actor. Or another Augustine on his way to a profound conversion. Maybe he was a budding St. Paul in the throes of adolescence. Don't be too quick to rush to judgment.

24. Led by Light, Not a Chain

Holy Spirit, you are with me since my Baptism. Yet how seldom do I raise my mind to your presence. Nonetheless, you are within me, forming and enlightening me in all the events of life when I freely let you do so. But you will not force yourself upon me; you lead me by a light and not by a chain. You call to my heart by the words of the Messiah, Our Lord Jesus Christ. You strengthen me and form me by these mysterious words which shape me as the words of the Creator shaped the waste and void into the living earth. O Holy and Mysterious Spirit, I am so weak and so blind, so poor and so much in conflict with myself. Breathe on me, O Spirit, and I shall be renewed. Touch me with your grace and I shall be made whole again. Enlighten me and I shall see all that blinds me. Lift me and I shall run in the way of your commandments.

25. Jesus Takes Up His Cross

A few years ago someone very dear to me faced the unspeakably heavy cross of having her only child killed by a prowler. What do you say? There was nothing to say. Unseen, unexpected, like a bolt of lightning, this terror came into her life.

And she said to me, "I read once that if we could see all the crosses of the world piled up, we'd take the one we already have. I don't want this cross. I'd rather be dead. But since I have been given it, I will carry it."

Maybe you have felt that way. I know I have. "O Lord, any cross but that one!" Today we meditate—and are grateful—because Jesus takes up his cross. We ask for the courage to carry the cross that comes our way. It only becomes sanctified by God's will when we lovingly accept it.

26. Don't Forget

Jesus said that he came to save sinners, not the just. He came to heal the sick and not the healthy. St. Benedict Joseph Labré is the patron of homeless people. When you pass one of these poor folks on the street, don't forget that they have their own patron saint who himself was a homeless and mentally ill vagabond for fourteen years. The church's arms are open infinitely wider to the huddled masses than are those of the Statue of Liberty.

27. Open to Everyman

There is an interesting historical parable about vanity. In Vienna the emperors of the Austro-Hungarian Empire are buried in a Capuchin friary. I suppose it was considered the humblest place to be buried.... The funeral ... procession would go from St. Vitus Cathedral down to the Capuchins. The grand duke would ceremoniously knock on the locked doors of the friary. A little window would open and the superior would say, "Who is it?" The duke would answer something like this: "Franz Joseph, emperor of the Holy Roman Empire, king of Hungary, margrave of such and such." The superior would say, "We don't know him." So he'd knock again. "Who is there?" "Franz Joseph, his most Catholic imperial majesty, elector of the Pope, etc." The answer would come again, "We don't know him." The duke would knock a third time and the superior would say, "Who is there?" Then the grand duke would say, "Franz Joseph, a wretched sinner who seeks a place to lay his bones." Then the door would open. Only in death do some of us face the need to divest ourselves of the world's vanity. It would be wonderful if we could get over our sensitivities sooner.

28. The Geographic Cure

Though we are all in a constant spiritual battle against worldiness and the devil, it seems to me that the biggest and most persistent enemy is always *self,* that dangerous Trojan horse within the gates. Have you ever tried the "geographic cure" for some chronic problem like alcoholism or depression—that is, changing jobs or moving to another city? The problem is, you have to take yourself along with you. You can never escape yourself; you can only change yourself.

29. Sex and the Key to Happiness

Perhaps one of the most persistent and obviously invalid assumptions of our civilization is that sexual behavior brings happiness. The media trumpet the message, "Sex brings happiness." If this were true, we would indeed live in an earthly paradise, and the world would be "Happy Valley."

I suppose that half the people you meet on a bus, or in a shopping center, or even at church on Sunday have had some genital sexual experience during the preceding few days. It is the observation of an old celibate from way back that they are not all so very happy. If sex brought happiness, the world would shine like the sun, at least half the time. Celibates need not try to convince themselves that chaste celibacy is the road to earthly bliss, but on the other hand they need not feel deprived of the key to happiness. If there is a single key to contentment, it cannot be sexual experience.

30. Working for Righteousness

Even though Dr. King firmly disagreed with the actions of his enemies, he could sit patiently in a segregated restaurant somewhere in the Deep South, while some bigot poured a bowl of sugar over his head. Rather than take the insult personally, Dr. King silently took the abuse because he knew that he was working for the cause of righteousness and justice. The newsreels which reported this particular act of persecution and the expression on his face—patient, yet profoundly disapproving—probably did more for the civil rights movement than many of the speeches he gave.

Too many times in history Christians have tried to be Christians in decidedly unchristian ways. But you don't produce the fruit of righteousness by behaving unrighteously. You don't promote peace by being violent. You don't further justice by being unjust. Scripture clearly tells us that the kingdom of God is to be inherited by those who are righteous and who act righteously.

31. Real Faith, Real Courage

I recall a frail little woman in her late fifties, who had few financial resources and a skimpy kind of job. She was telling me quite blandly that she was getting ready to go to jail for six months. She had given up her modest apartment, put her few possessions in storage, and given notice at her job—with no assurance that she would get it back. She later participated in a rescue at an abortion clinic, would not plead guilty, and was sentenced to jail.

While I agreed with her on the iniquity of abortion, I counseled her on some procedures that might protect the little security she possessed.… I stopped in the middle of my efforts to realize she understood something I had forgotten. Whether I agreed with her decision or not, she was very clear on one basic fact: that faith in Christ may bring suffering to his disciples.

If you find this lesson too tough to swallow, recall those words carved on that monument of martyrdom in St. Peter's Square: "Christ conquers, Christ captains, Christ commands. Christ delivers his people from all evil." We must not lose hope, and we must not run away.

32. Reverent Prayer

Let me be in reverence of your majesty and greatness and let me be in silent awe of your mysterious being and endless days. But most of all, Holy Spirit, let my reverence be like that of a child for his parents. Let me have the reverence toward you that loving spouses have for each other. Let me walk in silence in the beauty of your creation and see the fingerprints of your majesty on the sky and in the earth. Let me be deeply moved by your beauty when I see it on the face of a child and let me be most compassionate when I see your wisdom etched over a face marked with suffering. O Holy Spirit, give me your gift of reverence that I may always pass through life in a certain silent awe, knowing that you will have passed over the darkness and emptiness of the void and called it to life and that you call me to a more loving life in this world and to eternity in the next.

33. A Place for Perfection

A saint is just a sinner who is more repentant than most of us. If there is any place for perfection in our lives, it is perfect contrition for our sins. *Perfect contrition* is grief of the soul because we have offended God who is infinitely good, coupled with a firm resolve to cease offending him. *Imperfect contrition* is sorrow for our sins because we know we have been caught and fear the punishment due to them. Most of us are a mixture of holiness and selfishness, and hopefully we grow in grace and love of God as we mature in our spiritual lives. Some of us unfortunately never grow enough to take responsibility for our failings.

The journey to holiness begins anew every day when we begin to see some fault of our own, something we haven't yet given up. It can look like a seven-story mountain to us. We will despair of ever getting past such a huge barrier ... until slowly the grace of God shows us the only clear path over it. And then we begin the arduous climb, one labored step at a time.

34. The Spirit at Work

The Jewish people spoke of the Holy Spirit often, but it was Christ who equated this Spirit as a person with the Father and himself, making the Holy Spirit's relationship to the Father comparable to his own as Son, and so Christians are baptized according to the command of Christ in the single name of God, the Father, the Son, and the Holy Spirit. The ancient theological tradition of the Church sees the Holy Spirit as being the total expression of the love between the Father and the Son. In a word, the mystery of God as seen in the New Testament ... is a mystery of relationship in which the Holy Spirit is taught as proceeding both from the Father and from the Son. What is perhaps more understandable to most of us is that the Holy Spirit is seen as the source of the constantly extraordinary and powerful works of God in history.

35. Inspired by the Holy Spirit

Some are totally deaf to the inspiration of the Holy Spirit in their lives. They don't deny it, but it is something that happens to everybody else, it never happens to them. And so life is bleak and difficult and trying even though they trust in God and try to obey his law. The opposite mistake is made by those who think that all of their thoughts and inclinations are the inspiration of the Holy Spirit. St. John of the Cross used to say that he was terrified by people who went about proclaiming that the Lord had told them this or that, when indeed they were listening to their own imagination. How does one cope with the intrusion of the Holy Spirit into one's life? There are a couple of good rules. One is to be guided by the traditional and deeply spiritual teaching of the Church....
The great theological and traditional structure of the Church is the splendid guide which has led many Christians to great holiness and it is something that causes us to discern and prove the spirits which operate in our life.

36. A Second Rule

A second rule that one might make for the intelligent use of the inspiration of the Holy Spirit in one's life is to always keep in mind that whatever things we see or learn, be they from our senses or from internal inspiration, are always deeply colored by our own subjectivity. When you hear the purest message from God it is somewhat warped and fitted to your own ears. This is not because of any weakness of the message but because of how humans perceive things. Peter and Paul both struggled to be guided by the Holy Spirit and they arrived at different answers to the same questions. Those who make the guidance of the Holy Spirit an important part of their lives should carefully keep in mind that when five people read a Bible or a cookbook they all read slightly different things. It can be an intolerable arrogance to impose one's interpretation of the Holy Spirit's inspiration on someone else and be absolutely sure that one is right.

37. Spirit, Come Upon Us

Holy Spirit, you live in the heart of the church. Without your action, the church, indeed the human race itself would perish. As you did in the earliest dawn of creation and of human life, you pass over the world today and renew the face of the earth. Yet you, Spirit of Life and Love, force no one. You compel no one. You do not intrude. We wait for your coming like the apostles and disciples, in fear and trembling at what is going on around us.

O Holy Spirit, come upon us now in this difficult and dark time. Open hearts and minds to your truth. Strengthen our wills to resist evil and to do good. Give us eyes to see your presence everywhere, even where evil seems to triumph. Heal our wounds and undo the effects of our sinfulness. Then your church, your temple of living stones, will be seen as a safe refuge in the storms that break over the world.

38. God's Will and Success

It is commonly thought that if we begin a project for the Lord, the pieces will fall into place. It doesn't work out that way. One has only to consider God's greatest project, described in the four Gospels. The road of the Messiah was hardly strewn with flowers. It is good to recall the scene in St. John's Gospel (chapter six) when many of Christ's disciples left him after he spoke of the necessity to eat his flesh and drink his blood. How poignant is the question put to the few apostles who remained: "Will you also go away?"

Disasters befall projects of the good spirit, as well as those of the bad. Success has never been a sign of God's will. As Mother Teresa of Calcutta has observed, "God calls us to fidelity and not to success." It seems to me a sure sign that a certain project is the work of God if we have the grace to struggle on without bitterness in the face of difficulties and frustrations.

39. The Stability of Meekness

Sometimes the stability of meekness is what makes it possible for an ordinary person to face inescapable doom with dignity and faith. Many a martyr has done simply that and in death has defeated his enemies. But this is meekness in the worst of all possible circumstances. Even in the more commonplace challenges of life, meekness is a powerful means of accomplishing something worthwhile, of receiving more of God's light and taking that next step in our spiritual journey. Meekness gives an alcoholic the strength to get up at an Alcoholics Anonymous meeting and say for the first time, "My name is Joe. I am an alcoholic." That is exactly what it means to be meek. The meek don't seek excuses for what they may have done wrong. Rather than spending a lot of time defending what was ill-advised or sinful, the meek pursue opportunities to change for the better.

40. Survival of the Meekest

Scripture says that the meek will inherit the earth. Such a promise strikes our ears as rather grandiose, like hyperbole or grand overstatement. It obviously does not mean the earth in which we live; it means the heavenly world. Our reward for meekness involves spiritual realms, blessings that will last forever.

However, the meek do in a strange way inherit a sizable portion of this world. Do you know how? The meek survive. Did anybody ever say to you, "Oh, you're a survivor"? That means you have a basic kind of meekness. No matter what happens, no matter how terrible things turn out to be, no matter what disasters befall you, you keep trying to find the will of God in those circumstances and keep going.

If you're a believer who is struggling to make progress in the spiritual life, you already have a kind of meekness or you wouldn't still be trying. No matter what the odds, God will give you the grace to fight another battle, until the day is finished and the race is run.

41. A Disciple's Prayer

O Lord Jesus Christ, Savior and Redeemer, show me the real way to be your follower. Give me the wisdom and humility to learn from your words and from the church which you left after raising up disciples in your own time.

By your example and by your Holy Spirit, deliver me from following my own way, from constructing the image of you that suits my own needs and desires. Each of my inner inclinations can seduce me to construct my own image of you: my anger, cupidity, self-indulgence, arrogance, self-justification, and sense of self-importance. Like the apostles, I can have my own ideas of how you can save the world—but with my help, of course.

Break my pride by your humility, unmask my selfishness and innate paganism by your providential gifts that impel me to true conversion and humiliation. If necessary, let the knife cut deeply and let me not cringe back in cowardice. Let me know the true joy of your real presence; let me experience even in the dark time, the saving strength of your cross; let me be a source of your gracious assistance to those whom I meet along the way.

42. Remedy for Spiritual Sloth

[St. John of the Cross] notes that certain persons who have made some progress in the spiritual life (those he calls "beginners") may suddenly grow lax and tepid. They gradually lose interest, sometimes giving up completely the spiritual life, which then recedes into the past like a dream or an old love affair. If their career or profession obliges them to be "religious," such persons continue on but with no zest at all. The light of the illuminative way goes out and slowly they return to their previously well-defended state.

Often they become very defensive about their previous spiritual interest; they may try to distance themselves from it by cynicism and mockery, or they may grow depressed when recalling it....

The remedy for tepidity is obvious. In his classic guide, Tanquerey suggests that one frequently consult a good confessor, be fervent in acts of prayer, and, earnestly if not enthusiastically, fulfill one's duties.

Such a decision is the very foundation of existential psychotherapy and may, in fact, be the essence of any therapeutic process. Acts of the will undo spiritual sloth.

43. Reach Down, O Lord

Reach down, O Lord, and draw us to yourself. Restrain our evil impulses, open our hearts to good, to love, to forgiveness, to the fulfillment of your holy laws which call us to be like you.

Jesus, our Savior, knock with your wounded hand at the closed doors of our hearts and call to us in the streets of life. Give us direction in the confusion and cares of this painful journey. Stay with us, O Lord, for evening comes and the shadows grow long.

May your Holy Spirit fill the world with God's healing and strength beyond all our meriting or expectations so that we may be saved, and all those we love and the whole world.

44. Reasons Beyond Reasoning

The blunt truth is that much doubt is caused by intellectual arrogance. I have talked to dozens of priests, religious, seminarians, and informed laity whose grasp of faith was weakened and sometimes destroyed by brilliant teachers who took revelation apart but never fulfilled their promise to put it back together again. This was probably because they never got it back together for themselves. They were often caught in the most dangerous of modern superstitions. (A superstition is a belief which has no other foundation than the individual's need to believe it is true.) The most dangerous superstition is that the human mind can come to understand everything.

Blaise Pascal, who profoundly affected the development of science by his theory of probability, and whose ideas are the foundation of computer science, observed that the most important principle of human reason is the recognition of the infinite number of things that reason cannot comprehend.

Theologians and those whose faith is influenced by theology must have a vibrant appreciation of mystery and of the essential limits of human understanding.

45. Our Praying Mother

Everyone knows that it is the duty of a mother to pray for her children. The Church has consistently seen Mary as the principal intercessor in union with Christ for the salvation of the world. Pope Paul VI and Pope John Paul II both reiterated that Mary prays in eternal life in a mysterious way for all of those who are called to salvation. When trying to express this particular belief to an inquiring Jewish friend of mine, I was struggling with the idea that one human being could pray for us all in the mysterious domain of eternal life, in heaven. When I got around to expressing this basic Christian doctrine of the intercession of Mary and the communion of saints, stating that those in eternal life could help us on earth by their prayers and concern for us, just as friends on earth pray for each other, I concluded by telling him that Mary prayed for us all since she was the mother of those who were saved through Christ. He looked at me with a twinkle in his eye and he said, "Ah, I see what you are saying; everybody needs to have a Jewish mother."

46. Hail, Holy Queen

Early in the 1970s ... I gave up (I am ashamed to admit) the recitation of the Salve Regina (the "Hail, Holy Queen"). The reference to life as a valley of tears and as an exile seemed not to be in keeping with the spirit of those palmy days. Then one evening I suddenly faced the most shattering experience of my life. A troubled youngster with whom I had worked for ten years slipped into insanity and took his own life. I stood in the dark city street in front of our boys' home and there echoed in my soul the old prayer, "Mourning and weeping in this valley of tears, and after this, our exile, show unto us the Blessed Fruit of thy womb, Jesus." On that dark night the mystery of Christ was revealed to me as never before.

I discovered that this remarkable prayer had been written almost a thousand years ago by a man who was born so deformed that he could never stand.... The Salve Regina ... has been recited billions of times since his death, bringing hope and joy to those who prayed it in dark times.

47. Listening at the Liturgy

For most prayerful Catholics, listening at the liturgy means meeting Christ the Savior in an intimate, if mysterious, way. The act of adoration to the reserved Sacrament on entering the church, a devotion very much related to St. Francis of Assisi and his personal love of Christ, is the actual beginning of prayerful listening for most of us. Those who are uninformed concerning devotion to the Real Presence are deprived of a powerful psychological help in preparing themselves for prayerful listening. If one has prepared by signs of reverence on entering the church, and during the liturgy, then the genuflection of the priest before the reception of Holy Communion has much more significance. The adoration of the Sacramental Presence is a perfect preparation for the sacramental reception of the Eucharist which is an even more powerful personal experience of relationship with Christ. Communion then becomes a time of internal listening.

48. Be in the Presence of Christ

When receiving Holy Communion, we ought simply to accept, focus on, and—if I may use the phrase—let ourselves be submerged in the presence of Christ. Just *be!*

Soon enough, unless you are rather advanced in prayer, distracting thoughts will enter your mind and unwanted emotions will surface. Instead of trying to shake these off, I have found it beneficial to try to grasp one of these thoughts and look at it in the presence of Christ who seeks my sanctification more than I can ever imagine. Perhaps the distracting thought is a fear that has been troubling me. Silently I present it to my Savior, who overcame the fear of the cross. I share my fear with him in silence. Sometimes he answers me in a very subtle way. In my mind I can see a wounded hand, pierced with a nail.... In ways that human words are not able to express he reminds me that he once lived in this world, that he experienced these things himself, or saw his friends and disciples struggle with them. The Christ who waits in the silence of the Eucharist is mysteriously a Christ of flesh and blood.

49. Prayer in the Presence

A few years ago a very fine Protestant clergyman came to see me about a problem of anonymous homosexual contacts. He was married and had a family which he cherished deeply. The problem of homosexual behavior had come into his life only in his thirties, and he was deeply troubled by it. Not only was it sinful, but he was terrified that he might infect his wife with some disease. He had prayed, fasted, and made a retreat.

After a few sessions I mentioned to him that a number of Catholics have found a daily hour spent in prayer before the Blessed Sacrament to be of great spiritual help. He was intrigued by the idea of this time spent with Christ and began to make it a part of his life. He not only gained strength against temptation but his profound guilt and self-hate began to dissipate. He came more and more to a personal acceptance of Christ's love for him. Although he had gone through the adult experience of a second conversion or "second birth," he now experienced a whole new loving awareness of Christ as his Savior.

50. Mercy Calls Us

Mercy ... can express itself in an act of kindness, a simple word of encouragement, an expression of compassion or forgiveness. Nor is mercy limited to needy strangers: all of your friends and relatives can use all the mercy they can get....

Where can we get all of this mercy for ourselves and for others? God is our unfailing source. He promises a fresh supply whenever we run low. "Let us then with confidence draw near to the throne of grace, that we may receive mercy and find grace to help in time of need" (Heb 4:16, RSV).

Mercy calls us to a better life, to a way of living which is more real, more generous, more gentle, and more spiritual than we have ever known. If you want to act like a child of God and attain his mercy, if you want to imitate Christ who was most merciful, then you must practice this quality of mercy in your life and accept the grace to be merciful.

51. Through the Eyes of Mercy

What if you suspect that someone might be abusing your charity? Decide once and for all not to let it bother you, and then live by that conclusion. Better to take the chance of being cheated than to neglect mercy. Merciless people never have to worry about being cheated; they just don't help *anybody*. Those who decide to be merciful in an intelligent way should probably expect about a 12 to 15 percent loss on their investment. This is the amount I figure will inevitably go to charlatans or crooks or people who could be helping themselves a bit more than they are.

I remember a fellow named Scotty Brown, one of the few hobos I ever met who actually gave up his wandering life and got himself back together. This older but still able-bodied man said to me, "You know, there has got to be something wrong with every one of us who can't take care of ourselves." I agree. Something *is* wrong with people who can't take care of themselves. But it may not be their fault. We need to look at those who need help through the eyes of mercy.

52. Let Down by the Church?

To be let down by the Church is not a reason to leave her, anymore than to be let down by your family is a reason to give up family life and move to a desert island. Are there any who have not been hurt by members of their family? In his *City of God,* St. Augustine wisely observed that it breaks the heart of any good person to see that even in one's own home one is not in a safe place and that one may be attacked even there by an enemy posing as a friend or even by an enemy who used to be a loved one. If we all gave up on the human race because we have been hurt, we'd have to move to separate planets.

53. Faithful and Faith-filled

If you feel like an ordinary, everyday Catholic, do not underestimate your position. You may not feel able to do anything apostolic in a sacramental sense, but you certainly can be a witness in your own life, at home, where you work, or where you relax. You can volunteer to teach religious education in your parish and work hard at preparing lessons and teaching children and teenagers the truths of their faith. You can take a stand against pornography and urge people not to patronize places that insist on selling it. You can work at a soup kitchen or deliver meals to the aged at home. You could volunteer to be a eucharistic minister, especially for the sick.

St. Paul constantly reminds us of the many different functions of the church, just as there are many functions in the human body (see 1 Cor 12). Whatever your particular function may be, be faithful and faith-filled.

54. Teach My Reluctant Heart

O wisest of teachers and Enlightener of all minds, I ask you, Holy Spirit, to continue to teach me even when I don't want to learn. From you only good can come because you are goodness itself. And you teach me so much in times of sorrow and loss. You who are the pure light of all being can teach me so much in what to me seems darkness and injustice. I fear the shadows of the future and dread more days of sorrow and yet as I look back I have learned so much from you in the dark times. Give your comfort to all who seek you and to all who have lost sight of you but who nevertheless call out in their darkness. For the shadows will someday fall away and in your light we shall see light.

55. Take an Interest in Life

It is one of the anomalies of a fallen world that couples with children feel depressed because most of their leisure time goes into the care and education of their children. Single people complain that they have no children to care for and don't know what to do with their leisure time. I would always encourage couples to have some interest beyond their own home, however satisfying it may be. To a greater degree the single person needs to cultivate interests that are intelligent, enriching and, if possible, helpful to others. A productive hobby like woodworking or needlework adds a touch of color to one's life.

I always thought hobbies were a waste of time and a reason for going to purgatory. Some, in fact, are (e.g., collecting different ginger ale bottle tops). A good hobby, such as painting, is an opportunity for self-expression. It may reveal to a person the treasures of life which we seldom recognize. In recent years I have found amateur astronomy a fascinating pastime which I share with many other people. It is also a productive source of meditation and prayer.

56. A Legacy of Personal Reform

Modern society tolerates immense discrepancies between rich and poor, an atrocious lack of mercy to the unborn, a disregard for the physically ill who are indigent, a callous lack of protection of its youth against drugs and violence. This society desperately needs reform. There is a widespread fear in the intellectual world that we are heading toward global disaster, if not extinction. The individual feels powerless to do anything in the face of such overwhelming pressure. However, if even a relatively small number of people were to try to influence their own environment by following a Christian life of personal reform, change might indeed occur. It has long been alleged that Lenin complained on his deathbed that if he had had ten men like Francis of Assisi he could have changed the world. What would the modern world be like if Lenin himself had tried to be one of the ten and had approached his career with the values of St. Francis?

If there had been someone in Lenin's youth who had seriously embodied Gospel values as St. Francis did, the world might be incomparably better today.

57. Christ Is in Our Good Works

Those who attack the church and expose its wounds for public ridicule seldom talk about the tremendous number of works of charity which go on quietly in the church all over the world, including the Bronx [where my community lives]. Why should we stay there? Not because of anything we in our brokenness can bring. We are all nothing but poor sinners, cracked earthenware. From between the cracks, the love of Christ can shine out. We don't personally bring holiness to our neighborhoods. We respond to the presence of God, to the suffering of Christ in the midst of the poor. We are especially privileged to bring the sacraments and the presence of Christ to such bleak places.

As I scan my memory for illustrations of Christ's presence in the world through the church, I feel overwhelmed. Whenever we are willing to let Christ work through us, he does so. Whether it be the incredible works of the Missionaries of Charity in Calcutta, or the quiet embrace of the volunteer mother from the suburbs trying to help a little girl do her lessons, Christ is there.

58. The Personal Presence of Christ

Eucharistic devotions of all kinds are coming back. A legitimate question is why.... There is, I think, a historical reason that needs to be considered—especially by those interested in the pastoral life of the Church. We live in very lonely times. Modern people have more solitude in their lives than people did in the past. With the virtual end of the extended family, with the modern preference for privacy, with the solitude in the midst of a crowd that one sees as an obvious necessity in the multitudes of large cities—people spend much less time interacting in a personal way with one another. The impersonal one-way communication of the media now substitutes for the shared recreation and cultural activities of the past.... There are still great public events where people experience each other with shared feelings,... from papal visits to rock concerts—but all in all we live in lonely times, and it appears that the coming age of virtual reality is even more likely to be an age of the solitary.

It should be no surprise then that the mysterious and personal presence of Christ should have a profound human appeal.

59. Union Together

The word *communion* means the linking of two or more people in the same psychological reality. It may be the linking of people together in some heartfelt cause, or in the celebration of a loved one as with a birthday party, or in a grief shared as with a funeral. Communion can be said to exist on a deeply emotional and psychological level between spouses, friends, members of a family, or religious communities. There can be a kind of communion on the biological level, as we find with the mother and her unborn child. The word *communion* is generally reserved for positive relationships that go beyond the common needs and shared goals that characterize such institutions as trade unions or business corporations. Derived from the Latin *com* and *unio,* or *union together,* the term *communion* suggests a supportive and even loving relationship. A pack of thieves working closely together is a mob, not a communion; by contrast, the survivors of a concentration camp, meeting each other on the fiftieth anniversary of the end of World War II, reported that they experienced a communion forged by suffering and danger shared, even though they did not know each other earlier.

60. Holy Union Together

Religions often have expressions of communion, sacred unity, especially the monotheistic religions, in which one finds the communion of the children of a personal God, a heavenly Father. It is a part of religious history that Jesus of Nazareth placed communion at the center of the life of his new faith. Communion expressed the sharing of his good news, the Gospel. In a world of warring nations and combative tribes he sought to bring about a universal human communion with his prayer bidding all to call God "Our Father"....

Christ referred to the outcast as the least of his brothers (Mt 25:40). He said that whatever was done to them was done to him, a very powerful expression of human communion. He taught that those who lived by the Word of God were brother and sister and mother to him (Mt 12:50).

But Jesus of Nazareth brought this communion to a white-hot center of focus in the Eucharistic banquet, which is most properly known as Holy Communion.

61. The Leveling Presence of Christ

One reason for the Eucharist being a bond of unity is that it effectively removes class distinctions in the most authoritative way. All kneel in adoration before the presence of the universal Messiah and King. Already in the Gospel we see this in the case of the Roman centurion of Capernaum. His recognition of the authority of Christ would be remembered in the Mass till the end of the world: "Lord, I am not worthy to have you come under my roof; but only say the word, and my servant will be healed" (Mt 8:8, RSV). Only someone who has experienced the devout reception of the Eucharist at a Liturgy where the powerful and the weak of the world come together, as in a cathedral church or shrine, can know this leveling aspect of the presence of Jesus of Nazareth, carpenter and Messiah. It is a joyous leveling, not one inspired by law or constraint. It is a leveling of the heart.

62. Discerning Good Spirits

Often a person struggling in the spiritual life does not know what to do when a good project presents itself. Most of us have enough self-knowledge to realize that even our best intentions are never pure, but we cannot wait until we are angels before we do anything. It is a good idea, however, to wait a week or so to see whether an idea survives the lapse of a little time. Most great ideas are simply that—ideas—and like most seeds that are planted, they do not take root. If an idea persists in spite of our benign neglect we should, after a period of prayer, work out a plan for a pilot program. If doors continue to open, we should remain with the project. If permission is needed, and given even reluctantly, it is a good sign. A good spirit bids us make our proposals carefully and with a degree of detachment. A sudden note of egotism or bitter zeal in our voice may not be the signal to abandon the project; it is, however, as St. Ignatius suggests, an indication to review the whole procedure and see where evil has come in.

63. Using Sin Against Sin

Sin is ultimately a kind of madness. It is either a revolt against God and his love, or the rejection of his law in favor of some passing or temporary good. In the lives of devout people, sin is usually the latter....

The person who wishes to grow in the love of God must struggle against sin and try to minimize its effects in the lives of others.... We must be guided by the words of Christ, "If you love me, you will keep my commandments" (Jn 14:15, RSV). But we must also realize that if we are so deluded as to say that we have no sin, we make God a liar (1 Jn 1:10). Even the greatest saints admitted that they struggled with sin and considered themselves great sinners.

The question is not how to obliterate sin or how to get rid of it forever from our lives, but rather how to use sin and sinful inclinations to grow, how to harness the energy of our mistakes so as to use sin against sin. The challenge is to learn how to love much because one has been forgiven much.

64. Is Hesitancy Rooted in Self-Hate?

Self-hate in its less virulent form shows itself as self-disparagement or lack of confidence. I have chosen here to call this hesitancy. It is a hesitancy to do anything good or creative. People will often back away and not use their talents and appear frightened. What is really going on is self-hate in a mild form....

Hesitancy is quite treacherous. It may appear as prudence, humility, or lack of pride. Indeed, there are situations in which hesitancy is motivated by a self-hate that can mask a peculiar kind of pride. A person who is filled with hesitancy may sit on the sidelines of life and feel that the rest of the world isn't really good enough to know anything about him. Self-hate and hesitancy both lead to a kind of wounded pride. Though it may look like a virtue, hesitancy is not. When all is said and done, the Christian is a believer, that is, someone who seeks to take the kingdom of heaven by storm, a person who runs along the way of God and travels swiftly. St. Paul refers to the Christian as one who runs in such a way as to win the race. Neither hesitancy nor self-hate can be identified as a Christian virtue.

65. Refuge From the Icy Blast

You and I should take refuge in God's love for us from the icy blast of self-hate. Repeatedly we must remind ourselves that God has first loved us. It is extremely important for our growth to be deeply aware that God loves us. We should also be messengers of God's love to those who hate themselves. There are many people around who are filled with self-hate because they are unaware of God's love.

If I tried to link the struggle for mental health with the struggle for holiness, I would say it is most clearly seen in the terrible battle against self-hate in the depths of the soul. Once the chain of self-hate is broken, the individual becomes free to love others, to be generous, to escape from his own darkness. This is part of the mystery of God's love. God has first loved us; let us begin now to love him.

66. The Furnace of God's Love

There is a line in Sacred Scripture, *"Deus ignis consumens."* God is a consuming fire. We are consumed when we try to follow him. First our distractions are consumed. The thousands of distractions that plague us are swept away, and we come to care much less about recognition or self-fulfillment. We are drawn toward the powerful furnace of God's love. The fathers of Vatican Council II taught that the gifts of the Holy Spirit are given without regard to rank. Perhaps, if anything, rank and importance can be obstacles to the love of God. This is why you should pray for the clergy. We may have more obstacles to holiness than other people do. We could be foolish enough to take ourselves seriously and think we have a special place in God's sight. However, God loves everyone—Pope and pauper—equally.

Because God is infinite his love is like sunlight. It does not divide. You cannot divide the sunlight itself. It is all the same. You can hide from it or stand in the shadows, but you do not affect the source of light itself.

67. The Pride of the Angels

Pride is the beginning of all sins and faults. According to the Book of Genesis it was a desire to be equal to God that led to the fall. And following hints in Scripture, the Fathers of the Church believed that the fall of the angels was caused by pride. They speculated that it was the pride of the angels which caused them to refuse to acknowledge the divinity of the second person of the Blessed Trinity when they foreknew that he was to become a creature of this earth. They simply could not endure that the Son of God would be a weak and limited human being. To borrow a phrase from St. Augustine, they could not bear to see omnipotence become tired, eternal beatitude weep, and life die. They could not abide the knowledge of the Incarnation, and, so it is said, they revolted. No one knows for sure, but it is an interesting speculation. Certainly the disciples of Satan in this world have been singularly characterized by pride.... And it is obvious that when true religion goes off the track it is the result of pride.

68. Give Me Wheels

Pride sneaks down into the bottom of our soul. It makes us believe that we are something more than a creature. Pride makes us demand the things that are God's. It says, "I will not serve," or, "I will serve, but only under these circumstances," or, "I am willing to do everything you want, God, but could I make a suggestion? I'll carry the cross, but preferably something with wheels on one end, and a nice little shoulder pad." All these things are pride. While they may not be mortal sins of pride, they could grow into them.

If you have ever been a gardener in New York State, you know that no matter what you do, you will get poison ivy. You don't know where it comes from, but it is there. Life is a constant struggle against poison ivy and pride. Unfortunately, we can be seriously tempted by pride to the end of our lives. The old Irish proverb that the higher we climb, the higher the devil climbs, is true with regard to pride. Until the day we die it can trip us up.

69. Conversion That Keeps on Going

Every disciple of Christ is obliged to confess him before all men and to follow his example. This is the real meaning of bringing the Good News to the ends of the earth. The lethargy, depression, conflictful attitudes, and lack of commitment and zeal that are evident in the Christian churches at this time strongly suggest that no real sense of repentance and conversion is deeply present. There is no question that Christianity is losing ground because the Good News is not being effectively communicated to the people of our time or to young people who belong to families of faith. All those who consider themselves disciples of Christ must pause at this time to see if conversion is ongoing in their hearts. Every Christian is called to a ministry of reconciliation between man and God through the teaching and grace of Jesus Christ. We can hardly be working on this ministry of reconciliation for others if we are not pursuing it in our own lives.

70. Natural Virtues Heightened by Grace

The natural virtues—the consistent qualities of a good person—were outlined by the Greek philosophers ... long before the Gospel. These natural virtues are generally grouped under four headings: prudence, justice, temperance, and fortitude or courage. One or several of these may be observed in the lives of those who are far from faith or any real religious commitment. There are prudent embezzlers and courageous crooks. A devout natural man without grace will struggle to have a coherent set of values, although as Garrigou-Lagrange points out, this effort will leave him deeply unsatisfied. His goal—a decent, peaceful life in the shadows of this world—must leave his heart restless. The so-called happy life is intrinsically unhappy because of its very passing nature. In a person of faith seeking to love and serve God, these same qualities, or virtues, will be raised to the level of supernatural qualities by the Holy Spirit. The goal will no longer be the happy life but eternal life in union with God. Then these same good qualities will be properly called super-natural Christian virtues.

71. A God Understood Is an Idol

Mature faith … moves far beyond the dust of the desks. It is alive, vital, always searching for new manifestations of the mystery of God, always ready to bow the stiff neck of pride before the Unknowable One. This is childlike faith. The truths of faith, based on divine revelation, are the rock on which the mature believer strives to evaluate all the opinions, discoveries, silly ideas, fads, hurdles, and distortions of the intellectual world. The believer can be in the world but never of it, in the sense that he stands on something altogether different—the rock of mature and unquestioning acceptance of the mystery of God. He may question how other things in experience relate to this mystery, but he does not question the mystery, as Newman points out. A God understood is an idol, a projection of the human mind, even if that idol is surrounded by the trappings of Christianity.

72. Mystery and Meditation

A productive method of meditation is to place yourself at the scriptural event and ask: What does it mean to me? How can I respond to it? If by personal insight you are drawn into the event, the prayer becomes all the more effective because the imaginary elements will symbolically represent particular needs which you have. They may be far away from the actual historical event, but they do link you with it. For example, you might speculate about your actions if Christ were born in your neighborhood. Would you stay home? Would you go over to "the other side of the tracks" to see him?... These questions can bring the mystery alive for you....

Your meditation will be more fruitful if you let negative as well as positive feelings surface. For instance, you may want to ask God why the terrible events of the Passion could not have been avoided. This question may reflect your own resentment toward God about some problem.

73. The Instrument of Our Salvation

For the Christian, all adversities accepted with faith and love are called collectively the cross. We choose to see them and realistically deal with them as part of imitating the divine Master, who challenges us to take up the cross and follow him (Mk 8:34)....

Trials occur in every life, and the cross comes to all. Beginners in the spiritual life usually spend much time and energy trying to pray the cross away. And often enough God in his mercy lifts the cross of suffering, as we see our Savior doing in the Gospel. But trusting that God will lift the cross is only the beginning. The Christian making progress learns that in suffering and adversity there is much to be gained. Our Lord accepted his cross when his hour came, and that cross literally became the instrument of our salvation.

74. Make Christ Your First Teacher

As we pause to think of Christ as Teacher, remember that a person teaches, especially in moral affairs, much more effectively by what he does and is, than by anything he says. The entire life of Jesus Christ is the teaching of one who at every single moment was totally and absolutely dedicated to the reign or wisdom of God. Students of the life of Christ have said that at all times he sought to do the will of the heavenly Father. He even startles us by saying this in a mysterious way, by proclaiming that "I have not come to do my own will, but the will of him who sent me." If you wish to grow in your spiritual life as a Christian, you must make Christ your first teacher. Every one of the saints of the Church proclaims in different ways what St. Paul summed up so beautifully, "Let this mind be in you which is in Christ, Jesus."

75. Christ Forgives in Me

Every person who ever meditated on the Lord's Prayer knows that forgiveness is a very special Christian obligation. And so we struggle to forgive, but often reach only the desire to forgive, without real forgiveness. This desire and the attempts that forgiveness inspires are good acts in themselves, but they are not the fullness of charity. This remarkable quality is reserved for the person in the illuminative way who now realizes that there is nothing to lose and everything to gain by forgiving and wishing the best even for his worst enemies. Hostility is an immediate response to the fear of being hurt, the person illuminated by the irresistible and unquestioned presence of God knows in fact that he has nothing to lose. Then forgiveness flows along with mercy, understanding, and magnanimity, or boundless generosity. Not only can the person say, "It is no longer I who live, but Christ who lives in me" (Gal 2:20, RSV); he can also say, "It is no longer I who forgive, but Christ who forgives in me."

76. Forgiveness and the Imitation of Christ

Most contemporary psychological theorists are completely in the dark when it comes to real forgiveness. They may wisely counsel walking away from those who have hurt us or simply letting things go, or, to use the popular expression, "getting the monkey off your back." This is wise, but it is not the virtue of charity. Christ speaks of the virtue when he tells you to love your enemies, do good to those who hate you, and to pray for those who persecute and calumniate you. To the secular psychologist this may sound like self-hate or passive aggression. With faith in the love of Christ for all, and his universal will to forgive and embrace a sinful world, forgiveness is the closest possible imitation of Christ, who spoke of forgiveness of sins at the Last Supper, on the cross, and in his first words to his disciples when he rose from the dead.

77. The Challenge of Charity

It is possible that the Christian life of most of us has become boring and unfocused, even a dull burden, because we have forgotten the challenge of charity. Have we been lulled into thinking that the duty of charity is just a little extra responsibility of our life that we may or may not choose to do? The great obstacle to charity in our time is materialism. When most American Catholics were poor working people they supported a gigantic system of social agencies and schools. Now that many Catholics are middle to upper class, they do much less in proportion. As a group, Christians in the United States have been jaded by material possessions. We need to be reminded that renunciating worldly possessions and distributing one's personal wealth to the poor were required by Jesus not only of the disciples who wanted to follow him personally but also to a lesser degree of all who believed in him (Lk 12:33).

If God has given us his superabundant gift of salvation, we too must give to those who ask and must lend without expecting anything in return. And here, as with forgiveness, the motive is the love of God.

78. Help Us to Be Merciful

Holy Spirit, Spirit of Counsel, who can teach each of us to surrender our burdens of hurt and anger, help us to be merciful. Instruct us on how to read the hearts of those who need our help, our compassion, our understanding. Give us ears to hear the unspoken cry for mercy that comes from so many we meet every day. Help us to know where and when mercy is required of us as we make our way on the journey toward you. Teach us, above all, the freeing quality of mercy, the grace to be delivered from the prison of our wounded and self-absorbed egos. Grant that we may be merciful and that, at the end of our days, we may obtain that mercy which we so much desire and which we so much need.

79. Preserved Pain?

[An] effective way to defeat yourself is to keep alive all kinds of hurt feelings. The Pharaohs of Egypt used to collect their tears in vials and keep them in sacred places. They were buried in the pyramids with their tears. The Pharaohs aren't the only ones. If you want to live on resentment and hurt feelings, you'll have an unhealthy diet for the rest of your life, pure psychological cholesterol. How many people spend much of their energy lamenting, crying, being unhappy or sad or driving themselves literally crazy by living on resentments toward those who failed them? Yes, people do fail us. Some don't even know they're failing us; some don't mean to fail us. Some are so preoccupied with their own problems, they don't even know what they're doing. And some just don't care. The motto of the follower of Christ must be, "Keep going ahead. Don't look back." If our Lord Jesus Christ had been someone preoccupied with his own hurt feelings, none of us would have been saved. Mercifully, God does not nurse hurt feelings. For our own spiritual, as well as psychological, good, we must forgive those who trespass against us.

80. A Haven of Rest

A friend once sent me a snapshot that had been taken four decades ago, when we were in the novitiate together. The photo shows me as a seventeen-year-old sitting on a park bench talking to my father.... I was struck by how peaceful and contented I looked in the photo. I remember asking myself, "How in the world did this boy ever survive all these years? He looks so terribly vulnerable."

Survival at best—that has literally been my experience. But I have survived the swirling tides of life because I discovered a little harbor inside my soul—a haven that I didn't build, a refuge that I didn't set apart from the winds of life. Sometimes, in the midst of storms, I couldn't find this sanctuary, but I knew it was there anyway.

Because he is the God of peace, the Father provides this inner haven for each of us, a shelter that allows us to survive during difficult times, a place where we can receive the light of grace. If we are trying desperately to hold onto him, God will allow us to find this precious place of peace. He will hold out his hand.

81. The Burden of Injustice

God has especially called the Franciscans of the Renewal to work with the most helpless and pitiful victims of inequity: impoverished children. These little ones have practically nothing the day they are born and are given precious little in the days and months and years of their struggle to survive. They carry on their small shoulders an unbelievable burden of injustice.

You or someone you know may have been a victim of one of those children. I know many churchgoers who have been mugged, knocked down, hurt, and frightened by some human being who attacked them like a wild animal. I can only urge such victims to look back and see what might make a person behave in such a way. You will inevitably find that these crimes exist because thousands of children are born into a world without hope. I hope you will never be the victim of this anger and hopelessness. But if you ever *do* pay the price of victimization for the world's injustice, try to understand that you have borne painfully a bit of the cross, the same cross under which Jesus fell when he collapsed, exhausted, onto the streets of Jerusalem.

82. Loving Christ in the Poor

Christ emphatically identifies love and care of the poor with love for himself—both his humanity and his divinity. The mystics of the Church, all of them people of profound contemplative spirit, are characteristically identified with the oppressed, the disadvantaged, the poorest of the poor. This identification with the poor is often their most attractive feature to others.

Because the materially and socially poor are often noisy and distracting, even demanding, the care of the poor is frequently distasteful to those struggling along the way. They do not realize that it is this very disturbing aspect of caring for the poor that contributes to the transcendence of self and the death of narcissism. Ask yourself, Am I letting Jesus pass me by when I do not recognize him in the poor, the needy, the disadvantaged, and the oppressed?

83. Walk a Stranger Home

The great Russian writer Dostoevsky, in *The Brothers Kara-mazov,* suggests that we pray every day for someone who will die alone, and that we accompany them as best we can, as an unknown friend, through the doors of death. What a powerful thought! How real it is each day to choose some unknown person who will die alone and to accompany them to the throne of God.

84. Heroic Model of Calm

Some time after the secret onset of his terminal illness, Cardinal Cooke was to appear on television with a few mentally retarded adults in a charity appeal. He was so ill from a treatment that it was not certain until an hour before he was to appear that he could go at all. After the appearance the Cardinal greeted the studio staff as old friends, as he always did. Then he got on an elevator along with two sisters and the mentally retarded people. The elevator got stuck between floors. During the two hours that it took to get it down far enough so that they could crawl out, the Cardinal kept the sisters and their charges from getting upset by singing songs, telling stories, and saying the Rosary. He was the last one out of the elevator, with cameras and reporters all around. He appeared to be in great spirits and profusely thanked the engineers who had released them. He was, unknown to all but his secretary, desperately ill at that time. It is my impression that such emotional control in the name of charity should be called heroic virtue. It is clearly the imitation of Christ.

85. Take Yourself to Prayer

In your life, when things begin to fall apart, apparently by happenstance, perhaps because of the ill will of others, or on the occasion of terminal illness or death or economic insecurity or the loss of a position—when things start to fall apart, for heaven's sake, take yourself to prayer. Not prayer that is going to help you tell God what to do. That's not very helpful prayer. God already knows what to do. But prayer that will reassure you that you are in the hands of God.

86. The Embrace of Prayer

We have all experienced the failure of friends. For one reason or another they were not there when we needed them. We know that no matter what happens, if we turn to him, there is one Friend who never fails, who is always there. Our faith constantly brings us to that Changeless Friend. Prayer is essential here because it is the only way for us to encounter our Friend. He is changeless because he no longer walks in this world of change. Through him we come into contact with that multitude of friends who have gone before us to that bright world where he waits for us—his Father's house. Even if you have to pray in pain or agony as he did in the Garden, you will soon enough find him there in the shadows. Prayer, deep personal prayer coming from the heart of our being, is the way that we can embrace and be embraced by our Changeless Friend.

87. Drawn Out of Grief

You may very well believe (and you may be correct) that your wound caused by the loss of a loved one will never heal. You may be struggling to forgive a wrong and know that you will never be able to forget it, but the example of Christ can draw you out of yourself. The magnificent advice of St. John of the Cross speaks very effectively: "Where there is no love, put love and you will draw love out."

The first step in time of distress is to go back to your duties—to care for those who depend on you. This is often done with considerable reluctance. Depression dogs our steps as we literally drag ourselves around. A voice inside, the voice of the wounded self, cries, "Oh, leave me alone, all of you, and let me grieve or rage." Don't listen to this voice!

88. Kingdom Growth

Despite your destitution, your weakness, your distractions, your inner stresses and strains, do you feel the kingdom of God unfolding within you? You should, wherever you may be on your spiritual journey.

Not that this internal unfolding of the kingdom will necessarily feel like a beautiful rose opening in the morning sun, with each delicate petal touched by the dew. In reality, a great many Christians feel more like an untidy ball of yarn unwinding bit by bit, as if it were being batted about by a mischievous kitten, or like a knitted sweater becoming unraveled.

The fortunate ones among us may detect something profoundly spiritual deep within, be it ever so faint. In any case, you will know that the kingdom of God is coming in your own soul because it calls you to grow in holiness.

89. God Sifts the Wheat

How do we separate the good affections that are the beginnings of eternity and that will last forever from the good ones that will not last at all? To be perfectly honest, I don't think we can get very far in making these distinctions. No human mind possesses the depth and complexity necessary to determine what should be given up now, what should be held onto for a while longer, and what should be surrendered forever.

… I don't trust anyone who claims to know the next step in his or her own interior journey. Why? Because the spiritual life is not *our* enterprise. It is the work of *God*. He calls us forward by grace and leads us, one step at a time.

When we first respond to God's call we are filled with a teeming jungle of desires and needs, both noble and ignoble. Among the honorable ones are those that will last forever and those that will pass away. How do we sort them out? The answer is very simple: God will do it. He sifts the wheat from the chaff.

90. A Greater Faith?

How does one arrive at stronger or greater faith? By incessant prayer, which guarantees a favorable hearing (Mk 11:24). The parables of the unjust judge and the insistent neighbor are strong indicators that Jesus Christ expects his followers—you and me—to practice what we say we believe, even when we must persevere for a long time in prayer and suffering.

What more important message is there for an age needing reform than that both our minds and hearts accept God's gift of faith in Jesus Christ as our Savior?

91. Prayer, the Breath of Life

Prayer is the breathing of the spiritual life. No prayer, no life. Prayer is the way we speak to God, as well as the way he communicates with us. Without a life of prayer, religion becomes merely a set of human convictions, without any inner roots. For this reason our Savior not only gives us an example of personal prayer in his own life and at his death, but he also teaches us how to pray. He tells us to go into our room and close the door so that the Father who hears us in secret may listen to us....

We all need to pray, and pray better. A person who does not seek to grow in the life of prayer will, sooner or later, not pray at all. Those who grow in prayer will be sustained by it. A dear old African-American lady, Mother Moses, named thus because she founded a storefront church, once said to me, "I pray all the time. If I didn't pray, I just could not go on."

I think she said it all.

92. Blessings Wrapped in Newspaper

Darkness teaches us to seek God for himself alone and not for any personal enjoyment. It seems to me—and I cautiously depart from some traditional writers—that this spiritual darkness may be related to causes that are not exclusively supernatural. The effect of the body on the mind and the complexity of the mind itself have been better understood in recent decades. Often a true spiritual darkness is occasioned providentially by something that is apparently unrelated to the spiritual life, such as a dietary deficiency, loss of employment, rejection or the demise of a loved one, or physical illness. Certainly the great darkness of St. Thérèse was intimately connected with her terminal illness: profound depression usually accompanies the acute tubercular states. Wherever darkness comes from, it can be used to turn our hearts from self-indulgence and self-love to God. We should learn not to fear darkness or to run away from it. Most people who have been on the spiritual journey for a while have learned that life's best blessings often come wrapped in dirty newspaper.

93. Be With Us in the Dark

O Jesus, you who experienced and shared this devastated world with us, we trust you to be with us in the dark times. At moments, life can be beautiful and fulfilling; at others, it can be like a hell. Often, its dullness only leaves us weary.

But your Holy Spirit whispers in our hearts that you are here with us. You are not put off by our faults, our ingratitude, our weakness, even our sinfulness. You look upon us like lost sheep, like the prodigal son. You look upon us with pity and not with blame. You do not cause us to be lost, but rather to be saved. We cause our own loss if we refuse to turn to you.

Hold onto my hand in the darkness. Come to me in the lonely night. Guide me through the rough places. Help others who come to me to find your loving presence. Assure us all by your Holy Spirit that you are always there for us, O merciful Savior.

94. Praying With a Favorite Author

The question here is how to pray with a spiritual writer—whether it be ... Ignatius of Antioch, or ... Thomas Merton—and the answer is: Gratefully but carefully. Gratefully, because it is a blessing and a joy to come across a writing or prayer that expresses our own needs and experiences.... Sometimes a person may stumble upon a spiritual writer who will serve as his or her guide for decades. This happened to me as a teenager when I picked my way through an impossible old English translation of the *Confessions* of St. Augustine. I shall be grateful to that great teacher for the rest of my life.

Whoever the writer and whatever the prayer, all must be accepted with a certain care lest we inject our own personal point of view into their writings and prayers. Misuse of Scripture can lead to inventing a false Christ. The same may happen when we read an intriguing spiritual writer.... A writer is giving you his or her best; give your best to incorporate that message into your life, rather than idolizing the author.

95. Listening for Lessons

We can learn many lessons, some almost too profound for words, by absorbing the writings, prayers, poems or meditations of great spiritual authors. Sometimes they can be tucked away for years and then come to the surface as a real grace. We should be listening for such messages.

I once had the privilege of offering Mass in the cave of St. Ignatius Loyola at Manresa in Spain. As I paused after Communion, the well-known Latin prayer attributed to St. Ignatius spontaneously unrolled like a scroll in my mind: *Anima Christi* … "Soul of Christ, be my sanctification …" I had forgotten that I even knew the prayer in Latin but every word came to me effortlessly. I have found ten years of use for that prayer, often repeating it several times a day. I am grateful that I listened.

96. Religious Devotion

Devotion properly understood means a deep personal surrender to God in thanksgiving and repentance. In this sense devotion is a response to the command to love the Lord with all our heart, soul, strength, and mind (Lk 10:27). In recent decades the word *devotion* has taken on a pejorative meaning among some Christians. It has been seen as a purely emotional or subjective phenomenon related to histrionic or emotionally dependent personalities. Indeed, we do occasionally meet such people in the Gospels—Mary of Magdala seems to be one. It is worth noting that Christ treats these souls with compassion and responds to their devotion in a gracious and accepting way.

Devotion, however, should not be restricted to highly emotional kinds of people. Persons of great intelligence and ability, often illustrious preachers and theologians like John Wesley and Cardinal Newman, are capable of deep devotion. It may well be that what is needed in contemporary Christianity is a sincere devotion to Christ expressed in many ways for many different kinds of people.... Religion without devotion is a very dry piece of toast indeed.

97. Goodness Graced With Truth

St. Augustine powerfully and consistently taught that it required the grace of God through Christ to make a man a child of God. The modern reader again may have difficulty with this concept. It is, however, one that should be applied very easily to those who seek God with a sincere heart and have baptism of desire. In my own dealings with people who seek knowledge and others who seek wisdom I can easily single out those who have allowed themselves to be touched by grace and those who have not.

The latter may have a considerable amount of natural goodness about them, but they are not involved in truth; they are involved in knowledge. Perhaps the worst lies they tell, they tell to themselves. Inevitably, when I meet these people I come away with a prayer that since they are so close to seeking wisdom God will give them the grace to find it. On the other hand, one meets people who are somewhat lacking in natural abilities like intelligence or even consistency, but by the grace of God they have some knowledge of immutable truth. This indeed shows the mercy of God.

98. Victory Over Vices

This analogy [that the hart or wild deer killed serpents and then was very thirsty afterwards] illustrates much that is critical for the spiritual quest according to any classical author— our vices must be purged. This is the first step of the spiritual journey, and the earnest aspirant is warned not to compromise....

It is worth noting at ... the end of the twentieth century, that the struggle with vices is almost ignored even by genuinely religious people. Often the sincerely devout of our time seem to have little or no qualms of conscience about uncharitableness, detraction, calumny, and impatience especially if these vices have become part of the functioning of their personality and have become linked with the habitual way they pursue their religious goals. However good these goals may be in themselves, one is struck by the lack of self-knowledge and discipline even on the part of those who are devout. It is fairly obvious that some well-intentioned spiritual writers display little working concept of fidelity or loyalty to legitimate authority, which is really far more important than the selective observance of this or that letter of the law.

99. Start and Push the Limits

Mother Teresa once confided to me that if she had not picked up the first homeless man in Calcutta four decades ago, she would never have been able to help hundreds of thousands who are dependent on her and her sisters and brothers today. We have to start and keep going. We cannot all be Mother Teresa, but we can be who we are supposed to be. What we lack is the willingness to try and the trust to go on. I will not change the world or the Church—at least I hope not, because if I were to change them I would probably change them for the worse. Only God changes things for the better. But he does this through us if we give him the opportunity to use us. There is no limit to how much God gives us except the limits that we put on him by our self-centeredness and lack of trust. We must constantly be aware of the limits we place and must relentlessly push these limits back.

100. Elusive Holiness

One never arrives at the state of holiness. As a matter of fact, holiness becomes even more elusive as we make progress.

I could offer many common examples to prove this point. Perfectly coiffed hair is not something you arrive at forevermore. If you clean your house so that it's spotless, will it still be clean two or three weeks later? No, of course not. In even another few days, the dirt and dust will have started to accumulate again. Weeding the garden, clearing the driveway, or repairing the car or the house is a constant, ongoing process.

Holiness is like that. We never arrive at the state of perfect repair and purity. It is always out there ahead of us. There is always more that needs to be done. If you just completed a marvelous, thirty-day retreat, and then made the best confession of your entire lifetime, complete with a heavy penance … I've got news for you. The next day, you would be getting ready for your next confession. So would I.

101. God's Task, Our Task

Realize more and more that the spiritual life is essentially the work of the Holy Spirit. Our participation, although it may appear to be a very active struggle to do good—to "press on," in the words of St. Paul—is ultimately a cooperation with the Holy Spirit. Our essential task is not to do things for God, but rather not to resist God's trying to do good things for us. Holiness is his work. Our task is to avoid resisting him. Many people waste a great deal of time and effort doing what they want on the spiritual road instead of letting the Holy Spirit lead: they must do this, they must be there, they must learn some other things. This is not really following Christ; it is walking beside him and making suggestions.

102. We Are Always Becoming

Psychology is often not very helpful in matters concerning the spiritual life. But I do find it helpful in explaining this truth: in this life we are never finally something; we are always *becoming*. We are never stuck; we are always growing. It just may not seem that way sometimes, since human growth can be as imperceptible as that of the trees and grass and flowers. We may be becoming a lot of things—good, bad, mediocre, stuck, or unstuck—but we are always becoming....

Becoming holy is God's work in us. It has been said that our goal is not to be good, but to be God's. I think that sums up the struggle. Holiness is God's work in us which we grasp through faith, hope, and charity. Sanctification for the Christian is the work of Christ in the soul.

But it is always a becoming, a process, a journey. Holiness is always ahead, somewhere around the next bend ... until we round the final corner and come face to face with the Lord in heaven. We are becoming saints.

103. Union With God

It is not spectacular in any sense. Rather, it is like the sun at high noon in a cloudless sky. One suspects that if we were able to experience it without first being purified of all egotism and imperfection, we would be bored as little children are bored with great music. According to Augustine, it is a single Word spoken by God, with neither beginning nor end, and containing all.

Without being spectacular, the unitive way is also totally absorbing, like love's quiet joy. Perhaps human love, beyond its initial powerful impulses, is a good analogy, especially when one visits an elderly couple who are quite at peace and tranquil in each other's presence. Many saints have used the analogy of the love of husband and wife as a symbol of the unitive way. But human love is finite and time-bound; the only way for lovers to make it everlasting is to link it with the reality of divine love from which it flows and which it symbolizes.

104. Saintly Father Isidore

He spent several hours every day sitting quietly in the chapel in profound recollection.... He seemed to be oblivious of all sights and sounds, although if he were assigned to answer the phone or door, he would immediately respond. The novices referred to this profound recollection as "Izzy's trip."

... I asked him for the secret of his life. He at first denied that he had a secret, but after some coaxing I got him to understand that I was interested in how people prayed. His answer, which I did not reveal until after his death, contains, I think, the experience of transforming union. "Well, my secret, if you want to call it that, is not much. It is just sort of ... an imagination that comes to me when things aren't just up to the mark. It's come to me since I got sick as a lad, and it comes now often in the day. Whenever I stop to think about it, it seems to me that I have spent my entire life sitting in the place of St. John at the Last Supper."

105. Pray for Those Who Abuse Power

Our Lord himself issued a severe warning to those who abuse religion for their own purposes or those who persecute religion because it tells them the truth. St. John the Baptist was killed by a cheap political hack, King Herod, who had married his brother's wife. When John the Baptist denounced this scandal, Herod had John beheaded at the connivance of his wife and stepdaughter.

Let us pray earnestly for the conversion of our enemies, for the conversion of the men who killed the priests and sisters in Central America, for the conversion of political murderers throughout the world. Let us pray especially for those civil leaders who abuse their office to keep themselves in power. They have a curse upon their heads which is as old as the curse of King Herod and the curse of pharaoh.

I wouldn't want to be them; I wouldn't want to even be related to them.... I pray that they will be brought to repentance. But let us also pray for ourselves, that we will not fail to give witness to Jesus Christ in these unbelieving times.

106. Hopeful and Honest

How really hidden we all are from each other. "How are you?" "Oh, fine." We could be dying and we would say, "Oh, fine." When you are with the poor and you ask someone, "How are you?" and he's dying, he says, "I'm dying. I'm scared." In the suburbs when you ask, "How are you?" he says, "Oh, I'm fine. I have cancer of the brain, but I'm fine." We are usually afraid to tell even our friends the truth about ourselves because we are afraid to lose them. My friend Msgr. Bob Brown passed away a few years ago, but he was different. He was very ill and lived for six years with cancer. If you asked him, "Bob, how are you?" the answer would be, "Great, for a guy who is dying of cancer." The first time he said this I was speechless. We're afraid to share the very things that would bring others closer to us and us closer to them. We are afraid to share our sufferings. We might recall that our Lord Jesus Christ was not afraid to share his sufferings. He still shares them. That's what a crucifix is about.

107. Ready for Christ's Coming

As we know from reading the New Testament, especially St. Paul and the book of Revelation, Christians in ancient times expected Christ to return to judge the world, whose end would be in the foreseeable future. Obviously they were wrong in some sense, although two thousand years is just a weekend in astronomical time and not even very long if we consider the age of the human race. Augustine ... emphasizes, as do the parables of our Lord, that we ought to be getting ourselves ready. In a number of places he focuses on the observable fact that his hearers will be facing death soon and consequently should be using every day to get ready by living a righteous life.

In the sermon on Psalm 95 he uses the certainty of the last judgment to encourage people to live by the first coming of Christ (the whole of the New Testament) so they may get ready for the second. Unfortunately, we do not hear this very often because our age has chosen to ignore the reality of judgment and the possibility of eternal loss.

108. Opportunity in Pain

Jesus tells each of us to pick up our crosses and carry them. When we do, our long-suffering becomes a powerful prayer, an act of worship. We have the examples of our Lord Jesus Christ, our Blessed Lady, and the saints who patiently endured the cross before us.

One of the crosses that may come to us is that of a painful death. Thanks to the great strides of modern medicine, many of us face such an eventuality. The terminally ill rarely leave in a few days anymore, but often take several months to do what our grandmothers and grandfathers could have done in an afternoon! So, what should we do? Don't worry about it! A painful death could be a marvelous opportunity to pray for others, to surrender our souls to God, to prepare for eternity, to purify our wills and open them to God's will.

109. At Peace With Oneself

Most people who have struggled to bring chastity into their lives after a period of sexual indulgence report a remarkable experience of inner peace. The struggle may bring fearful conflict, but if the individual perseveres in chastity for several months or a year, he will experience an almost spontaneous sense of integration. The person is no longer at war with himself and, to use Augustine's powerful image, no longer suffers the gnawing anxiety of looking for sexual delight, and no longer scratches the scab of lust.

People also observe a greater openness to others and less fear of manipulation (or being manipulated). A person who teaches or preaches Christ's message will do so with new enthusiasm and conviction. The history of the Church contains the stories of clergy and religious who had reformed their dissolute or lukewarm lives to become foremost apostles of Christ. Although it is not said, it is my impression that it was the sexual reform of their lives which provided them with the energy and clear vision to work as they had not been able to do before.

110. Unexpected Forces of Grace

As we strive in life to be Christ's disciples, we come to realize that we do not in fact first love God; he first loves us. Chastity in married or single life is one of several spiritual struggles which reveal Christ's personal love for the individual. Patience and forgiveness are rooted in the long battle to be chaste. As we grow more and more chaste, we come to recognize Christ as the source of a spiritual delight that captivates our heart, mind, soul, and spirit.

It is important to note that the freedom of thought and feeling which comes to the chaste may open wells of repressed desire and feeling. The individual may then have to face unsuspected impulses and temptations; he or she may walk along cliffs of temptation and slip into chasms of desire. It is then that the gifts of the Holy Spirit will come to rescue the traveler and carry him on.

For married and single, following God's law and the way of the Gospel leads to a blessedness that nothing else can bring. Unexpected forces of grace come into play as the person is drawn to the Divine, and the two embrace.

III. The Laundromat of the Heart

We have only one life to live.… As we each make our personal journey, we struggle to "put on Christ" as the Scriptures say. Paul exhorts us to "put to death" what is earthly, and to "put on" compassion, kindness, meekness, and patience (Col 3:12).

Many of us fail to finish putting on the new garments of Christ by the time we die. Even when we toss some of our old rags into the garbage, they seem to creep back into the laundry basket for another go around. The Catholic Church holds out the promise of purgatory to those believers who die while still at the laundromat of the heart. We will have a time … to allow God to complete our cleansing before we take our place in the kingdom of God.

How many people honestly think that if they died today, they would … take their places forever at the banquet of the Lamb without any layovers? The majority of the human race falls far short of divine glory, even with the best efforts at scrubbing our stained garments and bathing in the grace of Christ. Thank God his grace and mercy extend beyond the grave.

112. Pray for the Dead

If you don't believe in purgatory, you should never pray for the dead. They would already be in either heaven or hell. In the first case, they don't need your prayers; in the other, they can't use them. Yet I have met many Protestants who do pray for the dead. Perhaps this is no less logical than our own neglect as Catholics. If we took purgatory a little more seriously, we Catholics would pray for the dead a great deal more than we do, just as we pray for our friends on earth. I'm a great believer in praying for the dead. Who knows what struggles they're having on their journey—even though they are already at peace, knowing that they are saved?

Everybody assumes, of course, that purgatory lasts only a few weeks, months, or years at the most. Why? How do we know that? Wouldn't it be disconcerting when we get off the boat in purgatory if our grandmothers are standing there to ask us why we stopped having Masses offered for them? Heed my suggestion: pray for the dead.

113. May Wisdom Teach Us

Holy Spirit, you create all things and all is yours. Yet you are so silent, so hidden that we never think of your supreme possession and disposition of all the universe. You, together with the Father and Son, create all things, rule over all, and summon all to you as our final goal. Deliver us by your wisdom in which all things are made, from all foolish thoughts of possessions and exclusiveness. Let us ever be mindful that we are stewards of all we have until the Master returns. May wisdom teach us to be generous, detached, joyous in giving, and careful in receiving. But most of all, Spirit of Wisdom, call on our hearts by joy and sorrow, in good times and in bad, that we may always seek first that kingdom that never passes away.

114. What Do We Perceive?

The human eye can perceive an immense number of individual objects in the course of a single day. But what do we really perceive at the depths of our being? Suppose a young woman dressed in a provocative outfit strolls through the local park. A man sitting on a nearby bench sees a seductive enchantress; another is vaguely aware that a stranger is passing by. A taxi driver sees a potential customer. The young woman's father sees his beloved little girl, while her boyfriend sees the most beautiful woman in the world. A prudish spinster sees only an object of disgust.

People receiving the same visual input may have quite dissimilar perceptions. This young woman becomes for different observers a temptress, a shadow, a possible taxi fare, a beloved child, a potential spouse, or a shameful harlot. A seeker of truth may perceive something entirely different, seeing only a child of God who is in danger of being misled and claimed by a pagan culture—and say a prayer for her.

115. A Good Dose of Mourning

I believe that most of us do not mourn enough over the loss of our loved ones. Do you remember how seriously Catholics used to pray on All Souls' Day for those who had died? No more. Unfortunately, the notion of the happy hunting ground has infiltrated the contemporary Church, and many Christians believe that we move from this world to the next without any accounting of what we have done with our lives.

In the midst of such spiritual confusion, we lose the ability to truly pray and to mourn for the dead. And when we suffer losses other than death—such as an enjoyable job or a treasured friendship—we don't know *how* to mourn. How can we, when we haven't wept even for the greatest of sorrows: death. Americans don't often become sad or sorrowful. More frequently, we just feel angry and frustrated. A good dose of mourning might really help to clear out our spiritual pipes!

116. Heaven: A Life-Extension Institute?

The great promise the Christian faith and the Church make to human beings is that they will through faith in Christ be brought through the doors of death into an everlasting life. The promise is given by Christ himself, by his apostles, especially by St. Paul and in that mysterious book at the very end of the Bible called the Revelation or the Apocalypse. Many people have trouble with this promise because they think it means a simple continuation of this life, a divine life-extension institute, as it were…. This is a very inadequate idea. It makes heaven into an eternal church service, and life after death into a hymn with an infinite number of verses. That is hardly a consoling thought. No matter what image of life after death people come up with, even one as magnificent as the one presented by Dante in the *Divine Comedy*, life after death remains ultimately mysterious. It is, as St. Thomas Aquinas said, "Totally different from anything we expect."

117. Live So That Others Will Sorrow

Not long ago I conducted a funeral in Harlem for an elderly lady named Vivian.… Her family was on our list for food baskets, and so they called me to do the funeral service.… I never knew the first names of either of these people because I always called them "Grandma" and "Grandpa".… "Grandpa" and I went to the funeral parlor together, and we paused at the side of the casket. "She was the finest woman in the world … the finest woman in the world." He kept saying that. At the end of the brief service, I got them to pray for "Grandma" on her journey. They thought it was a sensible thing to do. "Grandpa" came up to the casket before we left. So simply and directly he stood there with his hands on the casket and said over and over again, "I love you." It was beautiful and solemn. Don't forget this: someday it will be your funeral. Make sure you live in such a way that it will be both sorrowful and beautiful for those you leave behind.

118. Bring Us Home

Bring us home, Father, after the contest of this life. Bring back the lost sheep and summon those who have struggled even haltingly along the way. Open before us the great vista of the Heavenly City so that at the end of our journey we may look up and see its light reflected in the sky ahead. Give some glimpse to the eyes of our souls of that reality which eye and ear and heart cannot contain, so that we may not fail along the way as we follow your beloved Son on the road he alone knows and he alone can open to us.

119. In the River of God's Love

The love of God is like an infinite river. Julian of Norwich says the love of God flows like a huge tranquil river. Like the Mississippi or the Hudson, it flows with an irresistible power, and its deep current is unhindered. You and I are in the river of God's love. If we swim with the tide, we will float along with that love. It will bring us to where we are supposed to be. Then we will not be distracted, nor troubled by pride. But as soon as we resist, even a little, our going gets rough as though we are going against a river. First there are ripples, then waves. Suddenly there are cataracts of white water. We stand like rocks in the way of the great river. While we don't stop the river of Divine Love, we create a terrible turbulence all around us.

It is important to keep before your mind the river of Divine Love. The human race built dams against this river, but our Savior himself came and opened the floodgates. As it flows to us in that great river, God's love is dyed with blood, the precious blood shed by Christ.

120. Let Us Return to You

O Lord Our God, let us trust and hope in the protecting shadow of your wings. Guard us and bear us up. Bear us up, as tiny infants and into our old age. For when you are our strength, we have strength indeed. But when we rely on ourselves, we only have weakness. When you are with us, our attempts at goodness do not fail. When we turn away from you, we become twisted.

Let us now return to you, O Lord Jesus Christ, that we may not be overcome. For with you we find a perfect goodness which is your presence itself. We have no fear that there is no one to return to merely because we have fallen away from you. Our failures do not cause our hope of eternal life to dim, for you yourself are that everlasting home in which we hope to live with you forever.

Acknowledgments

Selections 17, 18, 52, 79, 85, 86, 87, 106, 117 from *Arise From Darkness*. © 1995. Reprinted by permission of Ignatius Press.

Selection 25 from *At the Cross.* © 1993. Reprinted by permission of Creative Communications for the Parish Inc., 1564 Fencorp Dr., Fenton, MO 63026.

Selections 97, 98, 107 from *Augustine: Major Writings.* © 1995 by Benedict J. Groeschel. Reprinted by permission of The Crossroad Publishing Company and St. Paul's Publishing, England.

Selections 29, 49, 55, 109, 110 from *The Courage To Be Chaste* by Benedict J. Groeschel, C.F.R. © 1985 by Province of St. Mary, Capuchin Order. Used by permission of Paulist Press.

Selections 10, 15, 34, 35, 36, 45, 74, 83, 116 from *God and Us* by Benedict Groeschel, CFR, Copyright © 1982, Daughters of St. Paul. Used by permission of Pauline Books & Media, 50 St. Paul's Avenue, Boston, MA 02130. All rights reserved.